Heartfelt Thanks Heartfelt Thanks Heartfel

Thanks Heartfelt Thanks Heartfelt Thanks

Heartfelt Thanks

for Sunday School Teachers

Group
Loveland, Colorado

Heartfelt Thanks for Sunday School Teachers

Visit our Web site: www.grouppublishing.com

Contributing Authors: Linda A. Anderson, Laurie Castañeda, Ellen Javernick, Karol Rarick, Donna Simcoe, Amy Simpson, Janet Welch, and Amy Whitesell
Editor: Jan Kershner
Creative Development Editor: Karl Leuthauser
Chief Creative Officer: Joani Schultz
Assistant Editor: Alison Imbriaco
Cover Art Director: Bambi Morehead
Book Designer and Art Director: Jean Bruns
Print Production Artist: Susan Tripp
Illustration: ©Susan Gross 2002
Children's artwork contributed by: Brianna Brolsma, Carly Flock, Stephen Grossman, and Madilyn Leuthauser
Production Manager: Dodie Tipton

Library of Congress Cataloging-in-Publication Data
Heartfelt thanks for Sunday school teachers.
     p. cm.
  ISBN 0-7644-2433-5 (alk. paper)
   1. Sunday school teachers. I. Group Publishing.

BV1534 .H39 2002
268'.3--dc21   2002011507

ISBN 0-7644-2433-5
10 9 8 7 6 5 4 3 2 1   12 11 10 09 08 07 06 05 04 03
Printed in China.

This Book Is Dedicated
With Heartfelt Thanks

to

_____

Table of Contents

Introduction

You are the one who answered the call.

You're the one who arrives early, sun or snow, to make sure everything's ready for class because *this* could be the lesson that leads a child to Christ.

You're the one who stays late to speak to the little girl with hurt in her eyes or to the teen with hopelessness in his heart. You're the one parents come to with questions, concerns, and occasionally thanks.

It's so much bigger than crafts and songs and retreats and games. You're the one who opens the Bible to them, who leads them to the foot of the Cross, who patiently explains, and who models grace.

You're the one who tells them about Jesus.

God called. And you are the one who answered.

Thank you.

Planting Seeds

I'm almost sixty now. When I was much younger and newly married, my husband and I lived in his hometown for a year while he worked on his parents' farm. I taught a second-grade Sunday school class that year. I'm sorry to say that after my husband and I moved away I didn't keep in touch with any of the children.

About thirty years later, our family moved to a new city. Shortly after we moved, we had an unexpected visitor—a woman in her thirties. I had no idea who she was; I figured she was probably selling something. But I was in for a surprise.

"My name is Judy," she said. "You probably don't remember me, but you taught my Sunday school class when I was in second grade. I live here now with my husband and my children. Some of the hometown folks told me you had moved here…" She trailed off.

I invited her in, and we talked about the people back in my husband's hometown, people we both knew. Then we talked about that country church where I had taught Sunday school and where she had grown up.

She told me she learned so much that year I was her teacher—I had made quite an impression on her. She said she had been fascinated with my gentleness, my love for her and the other children, and my passion for God's

Word. She had talked about me constantly at home, imitated me, wanted to be like me. In fact, she had told her mother that I reminded her of Jesus. And that, she said, was when she had begun to understand Jesus.

She had stopped by to thank me—and to see if I was still the person she remembered.

Judy's words were a great surprise to me. I had no idea that my teaching had made an impression on anyone, let alone a lasting impression. And I certainly had no idea that I ever reminded anyone of Jesus. I didn't even remember her from my class! But somehow, undetected by me, God's love had shone through me to cast its transforming light on Judy.

♥ Fill a paper cup with some soil. Plant a seed (any kind) in the soil, and set the cup in a sunny place. Or if you have a plant in your house, give it a boost. Move it to a sunnier location, remove the dead leaves, tie a ribbon around the pot, transplant it if it needs a change.

♥ Then read Matthew 13:3-9, 18-23. Consider the kids in your Sunday school class. Do they live in rocky places? Are they scorched by the messages of popular culture? choked by the thorns of hardship? Who are some of the children who seem to be planted in unfriendly soil? Write their names so you can be reminded to pray for them.

♥ When have you been discouraged by the results of your ministry?

♥ Where have you seen good fruit in your ministry?

♥ When you look at the seed you planted that's beginning to sprout or at the plant you nourished, be reminded to pray for your students and the soil they're growing in. Remember, God is faithful! It's up to God to produce growth in the lives of your students. He calls you to be faithful to plant those seeds. You may not meet up with one of your students thirty years from now, but you *are* making a difference!

Dear Lord, thank you for being a faithful gardener. Help me to plant the seeds of your truth and to trust you to nurture them into hearty faith. In Jesus' name, amen.

Train a child in the way he should go, and when he is old he will not turn from it.
Proverbs 22:6

Common Bond

As the teacher of a fifth- and sixth-grade Sunday school class, my husband wanted to set a good example when the lesson called for both the kids and the teacher to write down one question they wanted to ask God. He thought of a question that bothered him, and he wrote, "Why did my parents get divorced?"

When the students shared their questions, my husband heard the same exact question from a ten-year-old girl. Then my husband read his question aloud, and he looked at her. In that brief moment, the teacher and the student made a connection. They both knew what the other was feeling. A thirty-something man and a ten-year-old girl shared an emotional bond, and they both felt a little bit better.

What are you willing to share with your students so that you can connect with them on a very real level? The kids in your class need to know that you understand them. What better way to show that you really do understand than by being open and honest about your feelings and experiences? The more your students trust you, the more they'll listen to you. That's vital, because you're sharing the most important news of all! (And sometimes, as my husband did, you might just get a little comfort in return.)

Dear God, thank you for the comfort you give me every day. Please help me to be sensitive to the needs of others and to pass your love and comfort on to my students. In Jesus' name, amen.

♥ God knows exactly what's in each person's heart—the joys, the sorrows, and the hurts. And he knows how to touch each person's heart with healing. Read 2 Corinthians 1:3-5. Think about how God has comforted you recently. Then sit down and write a thank you note to God. Tell him what his love means to you.

♥ Pass God's love and comfort on to your students by growing closer to them. For example, you might bring in pictures of yourself when you were their age. Let kids see what you looked like, how you dressed, how you styled you hair, and what your friends looked like. Share a few personal memories that kids might relate to, and ask kids to share stories as well.

When I was a brand-new and very young Sunday school teacher, I taught a fun class of first-graders. Then one Sunday a new family, with seven kids who had a reputation of being wild, came to our church. One of the kids—third or fourth in line, I think—was Lewis, and he was in my class.

Lewis was very disruptive in class. I didn't know how to handle him. Not an assertive person, I was still quite unsure of myself, and I had never faced anything like this before.

Lewis and his family continued to come to church. For the next three weeks, I struggled to maintain control of the class—and to help my kids learn *something* about God.

Then some of the other teachers came to me and told me they would be praying for me. They knew Lewis was a handful and a challenge for me. They encouraged me to hang in there.

The next Sunday, Lewis began to settle down gradually. He started paying attention in class. He started to fit in with the other kids. I could tell that deep down he loved coming to Sunday school.

14

I was so encouraged to see the Lord answer those teachers' prayers for help in working with a difficult child—it seemed like a miracle to me! This boost launched my lifelong career as a Sunday school teacher.

♥ Prayer is powerful. Read James 5:13-16.
♥ How have you seen prayer transform someone's life?

♥ How have you seen prayer change your ministry?

♥ Your fellow Sunday school teachers need your prayers, just as you need theirs. Grab a stack of index cards. On each card, write the name of one of the Sunday school teachers at your church. Then go back through the cards

Heavenly Father, thank you for the privilege of prayer. Thank you for listening to us. Thank you for answering. Help us always to use this most powerful of tools. In Jesus' name, amen.

and write on each card something specific relating to that person that you can pray for. Use a hole punch to put a hole in the corner of each card, and place the cards on an O-ring, a key ring, or a piece of yarn.

♥ Put the set of cards where you'll have them handy. Flip through them, and pray through some of them every day. Oh, and you might want to add other people and prayer requests to this set of cards.

♥ Be sure to tell the other Sunday school teachers that you're praying for them. They'll be so encouraged!

Touched by Love

Sandy wasn't sure whether or not she should continue to teach Sunday school. She loved the children, but she didn't know if she was a very good teacher. She always got butterflies in her stomach the night before she taught, and the preparation time intruded on her weekend plans.

Were any of her students' hearts ever touched? Did her presence make any difference? Was it worth the effort?

Then one day, Sandy walked into her classroom and sat down on the floor by some of the children. A little girl with curly, dark hair approached her.

"Hi, Miss Sandy," she said quietly.

"Hi, Annie. Do you want me to read you a story?" Sandy asked.

Annie nodded, and as Sandy reached across her to pick up a book on the table, the little girl put her hand on her teacher's arm, gently stroked it, and then learned over and kissed it.

The rest of the class went by quickly and uneventfully, but long afterward Sandy remembered the young student's touching display of affection.

Did she have the gift of teaching? Sandy wasn't sure; but God had shown her that he had used her to touch Annie's heart with love. There are many ways we teach God's Word. We teach with our voices, with our time, with our actions, and with our hearts.

Sandy decided to keep teaching. She had seen God use her to touch a student's heart, and she had also seen something else. God used her students to teach her too. God showed her that she was loved, not only by him but by the children, as well. Yes, she decided, teaching was worth the effort.

the children...

♥ Read Hebrews 10:23-24. Then find a prayer partner who will help you pray regularly for your class. Ask God to help you be sensitive to signs of encouragement in the hearts of your students.

♥ Keep a Sunday school journal. Write a few notes after church each week about how the class went; note what the kids said, what activities worked well, and what spiritual growth you saw. Write prayers for your class, and be sure to document God's answers. Refer back to this journal whenever you're discouraged.

Dear Lord,
help me teach
your Word to
my students
with the power
of your love.
Thank you for
encouraging me
when I need it.
Please let those
I teach always
see you in me.
In Jesus' name,
amen.

Wrapped Up

Each Sunday, I ask my four-year-old what she learned in Sunday school. Some of her answers bless me because I know she is understanding more and more about the Lord. Other times, her answers surprise me and make me chuckle. Such was the case recently.

When I asked her what she had learned, she told me, "When you die, they wrap you in toilet paper!"

I tried very hard not to laugh because she was so serious about her answer. I probed further and learned that the class had been told the story of Lazarus and had acted out the story. My daughter, who played the part of Lazarus, was wrapped in toilet paper. No wonder she thought that's what happens to people when they die!

I explained, as well as I could to a four-year-old, that Lazarus wasn't really wrapped in toilet paper but in strips of cloth. She liked the idea of toilet paper better.

The image my daughter gave me of a body wrapped in toilet paper reminded me of times I've felt "bound up" by problems, helpless, and alone. I need to remember what my four-year-old learned in Sunday school—that, with the Lord's help, I can break free of problems as easily as I can break free from paper wrapping.

Dear Lord, thank you for giving us freedom in you. Thank you for your strength and love. Help us communicate your goodness to the students we teach. In Jesus' name, amen.

Remember as you teach your students that what you say may very well bless the hearts of adults at home!

♥ Read Galatians 5:1. What does freedom in Christ mean to you?

♥ Your students' problems may seem small to you, but they can be very big to your students. To help them understand that they can give their problems to God, do the following activity with them. Have kids write or draw a picture about a difficult situation they have faced. Then have kids fold the piece of paper and hold it between their palms (as if praying.) Wrap each child's wrists with a strip of toilet paper. Have kids pray, asking God to help them with their problems. Then let them break free from the paper.

Hear, O Israel: The Lord our God, the Lord is one. Love the Lord your God with all your heart and with all your soul and with all your strength. These commandments that I give you today are to be upon your hearts. Impress them on your children. Talk about them on your children. and when you sit at home and when you lie down and when you get up. Tie them as symbols on your hands and bind them on your foreheads. Write them on the doorframes of your houses and on your gates.

Deuteronomy 6:4-9

Encouraging Words

A kindergarten student reminded me recently about the power of an encouraging word. I was having one of those days that we all have from time to time; I was feeling tired and overwhelmed, and I wondered if what I did actually made a difference in the lives of the little ones I taught. I had an awful headache, one of my students had just gotten sick all over the classroom carpet, and the To Do list waiting at home loomed in my mind.

It was at this moment that a precious, bright-eyed girl in my class walked over to me. She just stood for a moment, quiet and still. Then she looked directly into my eyes and said in the sweetest, most innocent voice, "Mrs. Whitesell, God bless you," and walked away.

That was all she said to me. That was all she needed to say.

At that moment, all the frustration and self-doubt I had been feeling melted completely away. A few thoughtful words from a five-year-old left me feeling restored and reassured.

Weeks later I asked this little girl why she had said that to me. She simply answered, "I don't know. You're just nice, that's all."

Children expect so little from us yet give so much in return—just like a heavenly Father I know.

Dear God,
thank you for
the encourage-
ment I can
always find in
your Word.
Help me
remember your
teachings and
always speak
encouraging
words to the
students in my
class. In Jesus'
name, amen.

♥ Read Proverbs 12:25. Reflect on the words you've used with your students lately. Have your words weighed them down or cheered them up? If your words have been harsh, how can you be more sensitive in the future?

♥ Think about your students and the positive traits you see in them. Give each student an encouraging word in the coming weeks for such traits as honesty, friendliness, diligence, and kindness.

♥ If you'd like to go the extra mile, give each child a "character award" to celebrate the good traits you see in him or her. Look up Bible verses that relate to each of the character traits, and write them on paper stars or stickers. (Be sure to make extras in case you have visitors that week.) Present these to your students to show them how special they are to you and to God.

Transformation

Ronnie was not the most welcome sight in my sixth-grade Sunday school class. He wore T-shirts that advertised his favorite music group with bold illustrations of skulls, monsters, and evil signs. And his attitude advertised the bad behavior he used to claim attention at home and at school.

As much as he tried my patience at church, though, I was determined to show him God's love.

I didn't make an issue of the loud T-shirts Ronnie wore to class. When he chose to listen to his head-phones during class, I asked for his tape player; when he mouthed off in front of the class, we talked privately about what *respect* meant. If he didn't want to play a game, I let him sit it out. Sometimes Ronnie picked fights with the other kids, an action that usually brought a parent conference after class.

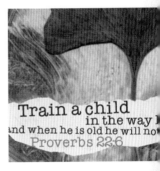

Train a child in the way
and when he is old he will no
Proverbs 22:6

Ronnie tried to act as mean as he could at church, but I saw through his facade. My constant prayer, even during class was, "God, how can I possibly break through into his world to show him your unconditional love?"

I set classroom boundaries and focused on creating a loving family unit with the kids. I concentrated especially on Ronnie. I invited myself to his house, met his parents, and began spending a little time with him. During the course of that year, we seemed to fight many uphill battles, but I clung to the hope that somehow, some way, God would reveal his love for Ronnie.

Then Ronnie began to ask honest questions instead of trying to be funny. I began to see that I was making a difference. I treasured those moments—the window to an open heart before God. The memory of those moments has given me encouragement through the years of teaching so many other children.

Two years later, Ronnie stopped me in the church parking lot. To my surprise, Ronnie gave me a big hug and asked me to forgive him for all the trouble he caused while he was in my class. He proudly announced that he gave his heart to Jesus and wanted his life to change. He thanked me for loving him even though he was "so bad" in class.

Later, I saw for myself and heard from the youth pastor that changes were taking place in Ronnie. Ronnie no longer wore T-shirts with evil symbols on them; he didn't talk back or pick on other kids in class. He listened to his youth leaders more, participated, and asked questions He brought his

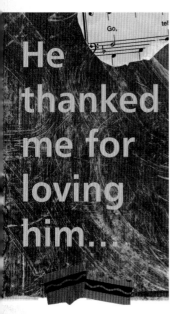

He thanked me for loving him...

Bible instead of his tape player to church.

The biggest surprise was the phone call I received more than ten years later. Ronnie found our name in the phone book and just wanted to call to thank us again for our faithfulness in not giving up on him. He had a good job and was married—and he was the proud dad of a new baby. He had continued in his commitment to Christ and was actively involved in his church. This one-time "nightmare" student had become evidence of God's grace and promise.

I thank the Lord for the privilege of teaching his children. He certainly accomplished his purpose in Ronnie's life, and he changed me in the process.

♥ Read Isaiah 55:10-11. What purpose does God have for you as a teacher? What are some attitudes or things God might be trying to change in your life as you teach his children?

♥ Choose one child a month and visit him or her at home—meet the parents and find out what the child likes to do in his or her spare time. Perhaps you can attend a sporting event to cheer the child on or just take the child out for a soda or ice cream cone.

♥ God's Word never returns empty. The next time you feel like giving up because of a "Ronnie" in your class, start making notes about the times he or she shows openness toward God. Document the good times, continue in prayer, and watch how God makes a difference in you and the children in your class.

Dear Lord, help me to treat the children you've entrusted to me with love and patience. Thank you for forgiving me and loving me when I don't want to follow in your ways. Help me extend your grace to the children I serve. In Jesus' name, amen.

"...so is my word that goes out from my mouth: It will not return to me empty but will accomplish what I desire and achieve the purpose for which I sent it." Isaiah 55:11

Hugs

One day I asked my daughter, "What's your favorite thing about God?"

She replied that God loved her and that he and Jesus were in her heart. Then she told me that they were hugging each other because they loved each other. Isn't that a priceless picture? Close your eyes and imagine God and Jesus hugging each other. When I think of that picture, it's easy for me to imagine God giving other people hugs—including my daughter and me.

When I think back on my years of teaching, I can certainly remember some children who were more difficult to love than others. But thinking about how much God loved those little children has made it easier for me to love them.

The mental picture my daughter gave me of the love God and Jesus have for us makes it easier for me to share that love with those I might find "unlovable." How about you?

♥ Read 1 John 4:11-12. Draw a picture of what you think God's love looks like. Maybe it's a scene from nature, a child's face, or a cross.

♥ Keep the picture somewhere in your classroom as a personal reminder to pass on God's love to those who might be difficult to love.

Dear Lord, thank you for loving us. We don't deserve your love, nor can we even comprehend its magnitude. Help us show your love to others—to comfort them in sorrow, laugh for joy with them, and over-whelm them with care—as you show your love to us. In Jesus' name, amen.

I See You

If you're a man who serves in children's ministry, you probably already know that there aren't very many like you. God has made you very special to be able to touch the hearts and lives of his children. Some of the men in children's ministry are single. Some are dads, and some are grandfathers or seniors. You are all so willing to love and serve. Thank you for loving God's children!

When I look for you in the nursery, I'm likely to find you walking a sleeping (finally!) baby in the halls. In the toddlers' classes, you're usually the teacher who is hidden under a pile of giggling children. You're the preschool teacher who uses tables and chairs to build "Mount Sinai" and then helps the children pretend to be Moses climbing Mount Sinai to receive the Ten Commandments. In the elementary classes you might be found behind a puppet stage dramatizing a Bible story or outside leading a group game that reinforces the point of the Bible story.

The children who don't have dads around tend to listen just a little bit closer to what you have to say. Sometimes just your presence seems to calm a discipline situation a little faster. Kids want to be with you—even when church is over! You might even be found during the week going the extra mile and attending a child's T-ball or soccer game.

Every time I see you playing, teaching, and loving the children, I can't help but imagine that Jesus must have cared for and spent time with the children around him just as you do.

Jesus was a man who loved and cared for children. No matter what your role in ministry, you show the children a "virtual reality" of Jesus. Thank you!

♥ Read Luke 18:15-17. What does it mean to receive the kingdom of God as a child? Write a prayer asking God to give you a more childlike faith and trust in him.

♥ This week, welcome children into your life. Find out what sports or activities the children in your class enjoy. Ask parents if you can come to watch their kids' games. If sports are not your thing, find something that you and a child have in common, and ask the parent if you can come to the child's house and share that activity with him or her. Maybe you'll ride bikes to a nearby ice cream shop or park. To protect the child and yourself, invite one of the parents to join you. Just be careful that the time is the child's time; don't spend it talking with the parent. (Save that for another visit.)

Father, thank you for the privilege of being an example of your love to the children I serve. Help me welcome them into your kingdom and teach them of your love. And help me to be more like you every day so children can see Jesus through me. In Jesus' name, amen.

Special Delivery

The other day, while I was checking my e-mail, my four-year-old daughter, Grace, came into the room with a box. She gave me a big smile and said, "Delivery for you, Mom!" I carefully opened the box to find several pictures she had drawn for me. I looked at each one and said to her, "Wow! Fine art! It's just what I've always wanted." She stood and beamed at me for a moment and then said, "Well, there you go!"

Her response made me think about how often God gives us not only what we need but also what we want. I recalled a time I was teaching third-graders with a new Sunday school teacher who really wasn't comfortable with teaching. She would rather just sit back and watch the kids while I taught every Sunday. I sometimes asked her if she wanted to give teaching a try, but she always declined, saying she just wanted to "help."

One Sunday morning after a particularly stressful week, I really needed a break. My co-teacher arrived that morning ready to teach the class. God had given her a fresh desire to do more than observe on Sunday mornings.

Dear Lord, thank you for always giving us just what we need. Help us to trust you in every situation. In Jesus' name, amen.

This timid teacher was given a fresh perspective and desire to serve. She had an excitement and enthusiasm that the kids loved, while I got the rest I wanted and needed. God had given us all what we wanted and needed. So like a loving father!

♥ What are some of your needs and wants? Pray a moment right now to tell God about them. Then read Matthew 7:11 and rest assured that God will provide for you.

♥ During class, have (or help) kids make a list of their needs and wants. (Be sure your students understand the difference.) During the coming weeks, pray for the concerns kids listed, and keep an account of how God answers your prayers. Praise God for his faithfulness and love!

Jesus said, "Feed my sheep." John 21:17

Feed My Sheep

After years of attending Bible College, working in youth ministry, and working on staff at our church, my husband decided to resign his assistant pastor position due to a drop in the church's income. Struggling with the transition, he decided to answer the need for a teacher in the two-year-old class. He had never taught this age level before, but the familiar verse resonated within him, "[Raul], do you love me? Feed my sheep."

I was the children's pastor, and I got right to my job of training him. I gave him the curriculum, and over the next few weeks, he began getting to know each of the little ones in his class. They played little Bible games, sang songs about Jesus, and just had a good time.

Parents began to notice that their children weren't crying as often about being brought class. They began talking about hearing their sons or daughters during the week as the children sang parts of songs they learned in class. One day as the children approached the classroom door, I saw one of them jump up and down with excitement and chant, "I see Jesus. I see Jesus."

When he was asked what he was doing differently, my husband would say, with a huge grin, "Feeding the sheep." Then he would add jokingly, "When they get restless, I pull out the crackers and feed them."

If you ask Pastor Raul what he feels God taught him over that two-year, transitional, "feeding the sheep" period, he'll tell you humbly, "The children taught me how much God loves *me* unconditionally. I learned servanthood. I learned to love and serve God's people (no matter what their age). But most of all, I learned to never give up loving them."

♥ God knows you. He knows what you've been through and what you're feeling right now, and God knows what experience you need to take you to a new level of understanding his love for you. Write a note to God to thank him for his devotion to you.

♥ What "sheep" has God given you to feed? Write their names below, and then divide the list into five groups (one group for each weekday).

♥ Read John 21:15–19. During your quiet time, pray for one of the groups of children. Set out a cracker for each child in the group. Pick up one cracker at a time, and prayerfully speak the following words, filling in your name and each of your children's names.

[Your name], do you love me?
Feed [child's name].

♥ Pause and reflect on what the words might mean for that child as you slowly eat each cracker. Then record your thoughts.

Dear Father, thank you for the children you have given me to serve. Open my eyes to see what you're teaching me through my service to them. Help me to love them unconditionally—the way you love me. In Jesus' name, amen.

Hidden Treasures

Do you have a child who seems to seek you out after the church service? I do.

My "treasure" is Wesley. Wesley is a somewhat shy four-year-old who makes a point of finding me after almost every service, especially when I haven't taught his class. I can't tell you why he's chosen me to be his friend (I only teach his class once a month), but friends we are.

I make it a point to treat all my children as if they're special, so I don't think I'm playing favorites. But Wesley is a treasure to the Lord and to me—because of the quiet challenge he poses during class, his consistent smile, and his willing heart, I suppose. I don't always know if he's getting the point of the Bible story because he doesn't always respond the way I expect. He often responds to my questions with a shy smile as he stares into my eyes, speaking no words.

The one thing I do know from his actions is that he likes me, and he likes to come to class. My prayer each week is that Wesley will see Jesus in my love for him. When he finds me on the days I haven't taught his class, he gives me a high five and sometimes a hug. Then he proudly shows me what he did in class. And more often now he'll even tell me what he learned. "Me and Jesus..." he tells his mom during the week. "Me and Jesus got rid of the monsters!" Yes! Wesley and Jesus! Wesley is learning to love Jesus more each week because of the faithful teachers who love him dearly and continue to be examples of God's love to him.

♥ It's easy to remember the tougher challenges we have and unintentionally take for granted the quieter, more cooperative children. Make a list of the children in your class. Put a heart next to the quieter children that you tend to spend less time with.

♥ Read Mark 10:13-16. Are you taking time outside your class to show your children you care about them personally? Make it a point on those Sundays when you *don't* teach to say "Hello" to your children and find out what they learned or how their week was.

♥ Younger children place high value on drawings of themselves and their teachers. If you teach younger preschoolers or kindergartners, draw pictures of yourself and your children together and send them to the children this week. (It doesn't matter if you send stick figure drawings!) You'll be amazed at what will happen. Receiving a letter in the mail is a memory of love that children won't stop talking about for days—even weeks—to come!

Dear Lord, thank you for the many "treasures" you've placed in my class. Help me take time to show them your love even outside the classroom. Remind me to pray for them each day. Cause them to grow more and more in their understanding of who you are, and show them how much you love them through the other adults in their lives. In Jesus' name, amen.

He said to
them, "Let the little
children come to me,
and do not hinder them, for
the kingdom of God belongs
to such as these."

Mark 10:14b

Ella

When I was a child, my flaxen hair and rather effusive personality earned me the nickname White Tornado. I didn't just enter a room, I filled it with bouncing energy and endless chatter.

While I suspect I was considered a pest to most people, there was one person who actually smiled when she saw me coming. Her name was Ella, and when I was in third and fourth grade and at the height of pesk-

iness, she was my Sunday school teacher. During class my hand waved in the air constantly while I waited impatiently to ask questions and demand elaboration.

But Ella seemed to sense that I wasn't being argumentative with my endless inquisitiveness. I really wanted to *know.* She saw past the screen of constant activity and into the moldable heart of a little girl who was searching in her own awkward way for childlike faith.

The love she showed me through simple kindness whispered to my heart that perhaps she was speaking truthfully when she said God loved me too. I remember a Sunday when Ella showed us a picture of Jesus surrounded by children. He was looking into the face of one little girl and laughing with her. I said to Ella, shyly for once, "You're like that." And she was.

46

♥ Read Matthew 19:13-14. Can the children in your class see Jesus through you? Are there attitudes in your life that need to change so you can see a particular child the way God does? Pray for God's guidance.

♥ Is your classroom a place of joy? How can you create an atmosphere that makes your students look forward to coming to church? Draw a picture of what your ideal classroom would look like. It wouldn't have to be elaborate or costly—just filled with color, interesting and varied objects, and, most of all, love!

Dear God, give me words so I can share your truth with these precious children. Give me actions that make your love shine through me. Thank you for this awesome opportunity. In Jesus' name, amen.

White Paint

The morning had not started out well. My plans to take my preschool class outside to look for signs of spring were going to have to be postponed. Colorado's weather is always fickle, but I certainly hadn't expected a snowstorm in April. Boots that had been boxed up had to be brought out again, mittens had to be located, and coats needed to be zipped—all before I could even load my own children into the car to head off to church. The car battery, not liking the return of the cold any better than I did, sat silent until my husband came out to jump-start the car.

The education director met me at the door with more bad news. My high school helper's parents didn't want her driving on the icy roads. I'd miss her help, and I knew the children would miss the snacks she'd promised to bring.

Parents bringing bundled up children joined me in complaining about the dreadful drive and the hassle of having winter return for an encore. But our complaining ceased when Evan arrived. He burst into the room and crowed triumphantly, "Did you see? Did you see? God painted the world all white again!"

How had I missed it? I had seen the snow but failed to marvel at its beauty. I promised myself that in the future I'd try to see the world through my small students' eyes.

Dear Lord, let me sing praises to you as I observe the world you repaint each day. Help me to better appreciate your amazing creations. In Jesus' name, amen.

♥ Read Psalm 104. Think about the marvels of God's creation that you may have been passing by without taking notice. Take time each day to be alone with God in a natural setting, even if it's just for five minutes. Spend the time delighting and resting in God's beauty.

♥ Devote your next roll of film to pictures of God's wonders in your own backyard or neighborhood. Photograph a bird's nest, a flower about to bloom, and a child's face. Then post the pictures in different places (the car, the bathroom, the kitchen, or the broom closet) to continually remind you of God's glory.

The Power of Words

"Oh no, we're short some glue sticks. I'll run next door and borrow some from Cindy," I called to my helper as I dashed out the classroom door.

"Hi, Cindy, I'm comin' in to steal some glue sticks," I called as I opened the storage closet and quickly grabbed a handful of the small sticky tubes.

As Cindy replied, "OK, that's fine," another little voice spoke up.

"That's wrong, you shouldn't do that. It's sin."

I looked down to see a five-year-old, former Sunday school student of mine standing nearby.

"Hi, Caitlyn," I said as I turned to walk out, not exactly sure who Caitlyn was speaking to or what she meant by her cryptic statement.

"That's wrong, Miss Ruth," Caitlyn said again. "You shouldn't do that. It's sin."

This time I stopped to look at Caitlyn, still puzzled by her comment.

"Oh!" I said, as it suddenly occurred to me that Caitlyn had heard me say I was there to "steal" some glue sticks.

"Caitlyn," I said, "I'm just borrowing these. I'll bring them back when we finish the art project next door. I was just kidding with Miss Cindy when I said I was stealing them."

Caitlyn looked up at me dubiously with raised eyebrows and then ran off to the next activity in her classroom. I took the glue sticks, but made sure that I returned them to Cindy's closet when my class had finished with them.

I was amazed that young Caitlyn had been so aware of the teacher conversation, and I felt sobered as I realized how important it is to watch what I say and do before my students.

But my heart was gladdened too. Not only did Caitlyn know that stealing was wrong, but she called it by the Bible's word—*sin*. Where had she learned this term? Very possibly she learned it at Sunday school. And that's another reason to believe that what Sunday school teachers say is important!

Dear Lord, please guide and guard my lips as I speak before my students, both during class and outside class. Thank you for giving me Jesus, a perfect example of how to reach and teach others. In Jesus' name, amen.

♥ Read Psalm 19:14. Ask God to show you when your words have helped or hindered your students and others. As you think about the effects of your words, ask God's forgiveness for your mistakes and thank him for the times he has used you to reach others. This week, rely upon his power to make you strong in the use of words for his kingdom.

♥ Think about a time God used someone's words to lift a burden you carried, convict your heart, or brighten your day. Jot a note of thanks or encouragement to whoever spoke the words to help that person know that his or her words made a difference in your life.

Guidance From God

"And, Lord," I prayed, "help Sammy be calm and listen to the Bible story today. *Please* help him say the prayer with the other children and not be disrespectful and distracting. Help me know how to deal with him."

I finished my prayer as I got out of bed Sunday morning. I was glad Sammy had good attendance at Sunday school and glad that he seemed to enjoy himself, but I didn't want him to distract the other children by making silly remarks during the prayer. "How can I correct him without robbing him of his joy?" I kept wondering.

During class that morning, my lesson went well. I covertly asked a helper to sit right next to Sammy. Then came snack time. As the children each took a seat at the table, an idea occurred to me. I decided to try something different. At the last moment before saying our usual prayer together, I walked over and knelt down beside Sammy's chair. Then I put my arm around his shoulders and asked him to help me lead the prayer.

Sammy looked startled for a moment and then proud as he glanced at his classmates. As the class finished the prayer, I was amazed at how well Sammy did. He spoke each word loud and strong. I had never heard him say it better. "Thank you, God," I whispered.

The tough kids are no challenge for God. He knows their needs and their ways. I have to remember to seek his wisdom as I think of each child and plan every lesson.

Thank you God for this day

♥ Plan a prayer meeting with other teachers before church on Sundays to pray for your classes. Be sure to share answers to your prayers and positive growth you see in your students!

♥ Read Proverbs 3:6. Then write the names of the children in your class below. Each day, pray for the children and for God's guidance as you teach them. As you see them make progress in their actions and attitudes, document the progress beside their names.

Dear Lord, teach me your ways. Let me speak with your wisdom and act with your kindness. Please keep my paths straight as I teach these students about you. In Jesus' name, amen.

"Rejoice with those who rejoice; mourn with those who mourn."

Romans 12:15

A Time for Everything

Our lesson that day was on Ecclesiastes 3. I'd read my fifth graders the version in *The Youth Bible,* and they'd really gotten into the idea of writing their own parallels—for example, a time to stay up late and a time to go to bed early. Because they were productively busy, I had time to think of my schedule for the evening. How could I ever get everything done? One thing was certain: I couldn't linger after class to chat with any of the children.

I got everything ready so I'd be able to follow the children out the door after our closing prayer. "See you next week," I called as they headed off. The only problem was that they didn't all head off. Sarah lingered. I stood with my hand on the light switch. She seemed to want to talk. I really didn't have time. "Gotta get going," I said.

Tears filled her eyes. "I hoped you'd have some time," she said softly. "Usually I talk to my mom and dad about tough things, but this time the tough thing is that they're getting divorced."

I sat down. It was a time to listen.

Dear Lord, thank you for always listening to us and caring for us. Please help me listen to my students and be there for them when they need me. Help me show them that they have a heavenly Father who will never fail them. In Jesus' name, amen.

♥ Read Romans 12:10-13. Then make a list of ways you can be more devoted to your students. The following ideas might help you get started.

♥ Schedule an individual "touch base" with each of your students, just to ask how each student is doing.

♥ Write a brief letter to each of your students, detailing what you appreciate about him or her.

♥ Talk to your students or their parents about what extracurricular events kids will be involved in during the coming weeks. If possible, attend those events, or at least ask your students for updates.

The "Gift" of Teaching

How many times have you heard someone remark, "But I don't have the gift of teaching"? Some people just seem to be born with gifts and talents that are obvious to everyone. Other individuals have to discover God's gifts within them. Providing volunteers with opportunities to discover their gifts was part of my job as children's pastor. Leading volunteers to this discovery was certainly what I needed to do for Tim and Betty.

What brought Tim and Betty to our preschool department was mostly a sense of obligation and a response to the need they saw in our church. Our church was growing faster than we could keep up with, and their son's class of three-year-olds needed a teacher for the next quarter. No one else volunteered. (Sound familiar?)

Tim and Betty came to the training session. (They were a little reluctant, but they were there.) I gave them the teacher guide and sent them into the class of three-year-olds.

The couple possessed a willing attitude to serve the Lord, and I was grateful for that! Each week, as I thanked them for the love they showed the children and tried to encourage them, they made it a point to remind me that they didn't have the "gift" of teaching and that they were waiting for someone who did to take over the class.

They may not have seen any change, but after a few weeks, I began to see their teaching gifts.

They had agreed between themselves that Betty would be the lead teacher. She would teach the Bible story and guide the rest of the activities. Tim would "just assist." He would greet the children, make sure they were signed in properly, and perform the puppet show.

One Sunday morning as I was making my rounds, I peeked into their classroom. Tim was kneeling behind a counter with a lamb puppet on his hand. Hidden behind the counter and reading the puppet skit with great intensity, Tim was unaware of my presence and the children's joyful response to the animated puppet. I saw, too, that Betty was good at keeping the children focused and keeping the class as organized as a class for three-year-olds can be. She also had a wonderful way of involving the children in the Bible story.

I commented on the couple's successes, but it took many months to convince Tim and Betty that they were making a difference in the children's lives. Over the years, though, Tim and Betty have continued to do some of the teaching in our preschool department. What started out simply as willingness to serve wherever they were needed has grown into an ability to show God's love to little children. Tim and Betty still won't admit that they have the "gift" of teaching, but what does it matter? They *do* have the gift of loving!

♥ Read Matthew 7:9-12. What good gifts has God given you in your ministry? How can you give good spiritual gifts to the children you teach?

♥ During the next month, make it a point to reach out and thank the volunteers, especially the new volunteers, in your children's ministry. Thank them for their willingness to make a difference as they serve God's children with their gifts.

Dear God, I know that your desire is to give good gifts to me. Give me the gifts you think are best for me, and teach me how to use them to bless your children. Please use even the talents and gifts I don't know I have to make a difference in the lives of the children I serve. In Jesus' name, amen.

Ask and it will be given to you;

seek and you will find;

knock and the door will be opened to you.

Matthew 7:7

God's House

I felt like a mother duck with little ducklings in tow as we walked from the Sunday school building to the "big church." I'd left my high school helper to straighten up our classroom, so I was loaded down with supplies for the project we'd do to reinforce the idea that the church is God's house. We'd already talked about how the altar is God's table, and my preschoolers were prepared to see the sunlight shining through the stained glass windows of God's house, just as it shone through their windows at home.

We sang "We're Going to God's House" as we marched across the lawn. We looked up at the steeple, and the children compared it to the rooftops of their houses. When we reached the door, I realized that my hands were so full I wouldn't be able to open it. Harlan was at the head of the line. I asked him to get the door for me. Even using both hands, he wasn't quite strong enough to pull it open. He did the logical thing. He banged loudly on the door and called, "We're here, God. Come open your door!"

Dear Lord, help me to knock on your door with every circumstance in my life. Give me faith and comfort in knowing that you'll answer my call. Thank you for loving me. In Jesus' name, amen.

♥ No wonder Jesus encourages us to receive the kingdom of God as little children. Is your faith childlike? What is one way your faith can become more like a child's faith?

♥ Read Matthew 7:7. Is there a circumstance in your life that you've been trying to handle without God's help? Do you need to knock on God's door, and know that he will answer? Turn that situation over to God right now in prayer.

Woman of Faith

After three services I was feeling completely exhausted as I checked all the classrooms and got ready to lock up the church. For the past few weeks, I had been struggling with the hopeless lie hidden in the questions I was asking myself. *Why don't you just quit and give up?* I wondered. *How do you know you're even getting through to the kids here at church? How do you know you're doing a good job as a mom teaching your kids about the Lord?* These were the doubts I had in my head as my elementary children's director approached.

She told me a story that will remain as a lifelong reminder to never give in to those doubts. Pam had taught my daughter's class that morning. She explained to me that the lesson had been about Abraham's continual faith in God. At the end of class, she asked the children, "Who is a person of faith?" Expecting the typical list of Bible heroes, which she did receive, she was surprised when my little Sara (not yet a first-grader) raised her hand and said, "My mom." Pam was so taken back by the unexpected answer that she couldn't continue the lesson for a few seconds for fear she would begin to cry.

As she told the story to me, I *did* cry! I certainly hadn't felt like a woman of faith lately. My daughter had seen something in me I had been too busy to stop and notice! "My mommy is a woman of faith!" she said.

As I listened to Pam's words of encouragement, I realized that God wanted me to see myself as more than just a children's pastor, more than just a servant. He wanted me to see myself as a woman of faith. God was calling *me* his *faithful daughter*. How could I possibly respond to such words except by humbly embracing God's love and grace for me—and never forgetting that moment.

♥ In what area of ministry do you feel discouraged? Read 1 Timothy 1:12. Pray for God's strength in that area.

♥ The Old Testament tells us that people built altars to commemorate times God revealed himself in special ways. These memorials were visual reminders to God's people of his faithfulness to them. Gather a few flat stones, a hot glue gun, and some permanent markers to make a paperweight memorial of God's faithfulness to you.

Glue the stones together, and use colored markers to write a key word that will trigger your memory for each time that God has revealed himself in a special way. Set the memorial on your desk or next to your nightstand to remind you that God is faithful.

Dear Lord, your faithfulness is too wonderful for words. I humbly say, "Thank you!" Help me to wholeheartedly believe and embrace your plans for me. Help me continue to serve you faithfully and believe that you are changing the hearts and the destinies of the children I serve. In Jesus' name, amen.

The Ultimate Sacrifice

I love kindergartners. I love their innocence. I love their energy. I love their faith. Amanda had all those qualities, and at the end of the day, I truly understood what Jesus meant when he said "...and a little child will lead them."

We were at the end of a series of lessons on how wonderful our home in heaven will be. Each week had included an explanation of how to go to heaven by asking Jesus into our hearts. Most of the children had responded wonderfully, and several had come up to ask Jesus into their hearts. But I could see that Amanda was feeling an intense struggle.

She always asked insightful, thoughtful questions about heaven, and she seemed eager to ask Jesus into her heart. But something held her back.

On the last day of our series, she quietly came up to me and said she was ready to go to heaven. She asked if I would help her ask Jesus into her heart. I found a quiet spot for us to sit, and she looked up at me with huge tears in her eyes. She asked if it would hurt, and then she asked a question that revealed the reason behind all her hesitation. She asked if after she was in heaven today if her mommy and daddy could come visit her. She thought that when she asked Jesus into her heart, he would take her to heaven immediately. She was ready to give up *everything* to be in heaven with him, and I was humbled.

♥ Few of us have had to sacrifice to follow Jesus. Read Matthew 19:29, and contemplate what you truly would be willing to give up in order to follow Jesus. Would you leave your house, your brothers or sisters, mother or father, children, or employment? Spend time with Jesus sharing your willingness to leave everything behind to be in heaven with him, just as little Amanda did.

♥ Spend time reading about Christian martyrs. Then think about what someone might write about your life and your sacrifices for Jesus. Finally, think of ways you can commit more fully to Christ.

Dear Lord, thank you for your great sacrifice for me. Please teach me how I can follow you more fully, and show me how I can lead others to understand what you did for us. Thank you again. In Jesus' name, amen.

Christ's Ambassadors

My mother tells me that when I was three years old I loved to go to Sunday school. My teacher's name was Margaret, and she was very popular with my class of three-year-olds.

Our church used the King James Version of the Bible, so we became familiar with its dignified language. God was "Thee" and "Thou"; "you are" was "thou art." Jesus said "verily" a lot. People "doeth," "maketh," "hath," "belongeth," and "crieth." To us, it was the language of church.

I don't know how it started, but for some reason we three-year-olds transformed the name of our beloved teacher into "Margareth." We called her by that name all year long. Apparently it caused quite a few smiles in the adult population of the church. They wondered why we changed her name, but we didn't have an explanation. Perhaps it was because such a dignified name just seemed more fitting for someone we so loved and revered.

♥ Even though it's lots of fun, teaching is a serious task. Read James 3:1 to see how seriously God takes it.
♥ Time for a project. Next chance you get, interview some children to find out what they think of their Sunday school teachers. List some of the words

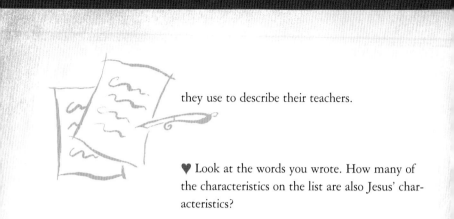

they use to describe their teachers.

♥ Look at the words you wrote. How many of the characteristics on the list are also Jesus' characteristics?

♥ How could you be more like Jesus in your teaching? Write three areas you could work on.

♥ Remember, you are a representative of Christ to at least one group of very important people— the students in your class! As you abide in Christ, he will be faithful and show his love through you. What an awesome calling and privilege!

Dear Lord, thank you for showing us what real love is. Please help me to pass that love onto the kids I teach. In Jesus' name, amen.

To this you were called,

because Christ suffered for you,

leaving you an example,

that you should

follow in his steps.

1 Peter 2:21

Promoted!

Kids *do* say the funniest things sometimes, don't they?

During a recent chapel service, we were discussing the story of Christ's resurrection. When our guest speaker asked what happened to Jesus on the third day, a small, pre-kindergarten student eagerly (and very proudly) answered, "He got a raise!"

I chuckled at the answer given so innocently by that preschooler, and I continued to think about it for the rest of the day. That night I began to reflect about it again and discovered just how true that child's response had been.

Often a raise means a person has been promoted—to a better job or a better position. When Jesus rose on the third day, he did in fact get a raise. He was "promoted" to a new and better place—heaven. We, too, will be promoted one day because of Christ's sacrifice for us. What an awesome privilege and responsibility it is to pass that knowledge on to the children in your class!

It turns out I learned two valuable lessons that day. One lesson I learned from a wonderful guest speaker; I learned another lesson from a four-year-old boy who reminded me why I do what I do. If even one of my students accepts Christ and is therefore promoted to heaven one day, it will all have been worthwhile.

💜 Read Philippians 3:14. What do you think heaven will be like? How would you describe heaven and its wonders to the children in your class?

💜 Have your students illustrate what they think heaven will look like. Read them Bible verses about heaven and compare their drawings to what God's Word tells us about heaven.

Dear Lord, I thank you because someday I will get a raise and be promoted to live in heaven with you. Help me do the best job I possibly can in teaching my students so that they, too, will be able to dwell there with you someday. In Jesus' name, amen.

75

Clean Feet

The year was 1937. Robert was the second oldest of eleven children in a family that was the poorest in the entire county in central Wisconsin. But Robert's family loved the Lord, and he never missed a chance to be in church.

One thing bothered Robert. Shoes were very hard to come by. Having no shoes wasn't bad at all in summer and early fall, but winter was tough. As Robert walked to church that warm October morning, he hoped he would manage to get a pair of shoes before the snow started to fall.

Rain the night before had left lovely, squishy mud puddles everywhere on the way to the church. What boy with bare feet could resist? Almost before he knew what he was doing, Robert felt the fresh mud between his toes. It was great! Then he heard the church bells peal. He didn't want to be late for Sunday school.

But what about his muddy feet? He tried to wipe them off as best he could, and crept quietly into the back of the room. He was terrified that the other children would see his feet. He got teased enough for not having shoes; if they saw how dirty his feet were, they would really let him have it. He tucked his feet under his chair.

Miss Turner started her lesson. She looked so lovely in her new, white, linen dress. Robert smiled at her and tucked his feet further under the chair. "No one must see my feet," he thought desperately. Suddenly, as he pulled his feet still further under his chair, he lost his balance, and the chair tipped over. Robert's dirty feet stuck up in the air for everyone to see. Everyone started to laugh.

Everyone but Miss Turner. She quickly left the room and returned with a bowl of water and a towel. She helped Robert into his chair and knelt down in that beautiful, white, linen dress and washed his feet.

No one was laughing now. Everyone was watching. Everyone was noticing Robert. Everyone had new respect for him because Miss Turner was treating him with such respect.

After that day, no one in that class teased Robert. And Robert remembered the lesson he learned. When he grew up, he carried a servant's heart with him. He served his Lord, his church, and his family all the days of his life.

Dear God, thank you for sending Jesus, the ultimate servant. Please give me a servant's heart as I teach the children in my class about your love. In Jesus' name, amen.

♥ Do you have children with "dirty feet" in your class? Think of the children in your class or in your church that others might see as unlovable. Write their names on a light-colored washcloth and place the washcloth near your sink at home. Each time you go to the sink to wash, ask the Lord to show you how you can wash the feet of the "Roberts" in your class.

♥ Determine an act of servanthood you can perform for each child in your class during the next few weeks. Keep a record of your actions and the children's responses.

I have set you

an example

that you should do

as I have done for you.

John 13:15

An Easter Gift

Easter eggs dotted the church grounds and peeked from beneath bushes. Preschoolers, baskets in hand, waited eagerly for the hunt to begin. Seth, our little Down syndrome student, also stood at the starting line with his mother beside him.

The director blew her whistle, and the children dashed off.

Like little birds, they chirped excitedly each time they spotted one of the brightly colored eggs. In less than ten minutes, every egg had been claimed, and all the children returned, baskets full. All the children, that is, except Seth. His basket was empty. He'd moved only a few feet from the starting line, and then, overwhelmed by the activity around him, had just stopped.

Abby, one of Seth's classmates, noticed he didn't have a single egg. She reached into her basket and took out a yellow one. She was about to

The joy of discovery on Seth's face was a delight...

hand it to Seth when his mother stopped her. "Abby, dear," she said, "that was kind, but not helpful." She leaned down and whispered something to Abby.

Abby took the yellow egg and ran a few feet ahead of Seth. She put the egg on the grass and called, "Look, Seth!" She pointed to the ground. Seth saw the egg. A smile lit up his face as he moved forward.

"Me find egg!" he said.

The joy of discovery on Seth's face was a delight to witness. As I watched, I wondered how many times I had robbed my own students of that joy by trying to teach and preach too much. I vowed that day to try to lead my kids to the joy of discovery.

When I was a child, I talked like a child, I thought like a child, I reasoned like a child.

💜 Ask yourself how often you do things for your students instead of providing them with opportunities to learn on their own and become more independent. What are three ways you can tweak your teaching style to allow more discovery in your classroom?

💜 Read 1 Corinthians 13:11-12. How is God gently leading you to know him better? What opportunities has he placed in your path to lead you closer to him?

Dear God, thank you for leading us, your children, closer to you. Help me know you better and pass that knowledge on to my own students. In Jesus' name, amen.

Thank You, Lord

Scooter was crying, and none of us could figure out why. The Thanksgiving lesson I'd planned seemed simple enough. Our four-year-olds were searching magazines, locating pictures of things for which they were thankful. Most children already had several pictures glued to their papers.

We thought Scooter would have lots of things to be thankful for. In his new foster home, he had many things that he'd lacked in his birth home. I was surprised not to see pictures of food, clothes, toys, or even a bed on Scooter's paper, but his page was empty. And he was sobbing.

English was his second language, so my sweet, grandmotherly helper checked to be sure that he understood the directions. He assured her that he did but kept saying, "Me no find picture." We were still trying to determine what he so desperately wanted a picture of when his foster family arrived to pick him up. His little face lit up at the sight of his new father and mother and sisters and brothers. He pointed to the magazines on the table, and said accusingly, "They have no pictures of them."

Scooter's words reminded me that parents are more precious than possessions and that families are the foundations upon which faith develops. I realized at that moment that as a teacher, I had the opportunity (and responsibility) to build upon those family foundations.

*Heavenly Father,
let me remember
that parents are my
students' first
teachers. Help me
support and nur-
ture them in their
efforts. In Jesus'
name, amen.*

♥ How involved are your students' families in your teaching? Make a list of ways you could involve them. Maybe you could have a monthly family fellowship time after class just to chat and compare notes. Or you could call one student's parents per week for a quick conversation about what you've been teaching and ways the parents could reinforce the lesson at home.

♥ Everyone needs encouragement. Each week, deliver one positive parenting comment to the parents of one of your students. Begin sentences with phrases such as, "I noticed..." "I'm happy to see..." "Thanks for..."

♥ Read Psalm 68:4-6a. Remember that families are a precious gift from God. Write a note this week to someone in your own family just to say, "I love you."

What's in a Name?

DeVilliers Frank Steyn. Such a big name for such a little guy. But what a great lesson he helped me learn that day.

I hadn't planned on working in the four-year-old room, but the teacher called in sick at the last minute. As the director of children's education in our small church, I had to fill in.

DeVilliers, who was named for his grandfather in South Africa, was new to the church. Having such an unusual name and being new to the church, proved too much for little DeVilliers to handle. So he came up with his own solution.

I had not been in this classroom much and was not familiar with the children. When I arrived in the room, I couldn't find the check-in sheet, and several children were already in the room with the high school volunteer. So I grabbed the blank name tags and went around asking all the children their names.

The rest of the class went very well, and before I knew it, the parents were arriving for their children. As parents told me the name of their child, I released the child to the parent happily. Then DeVilliers' parents arrived. They politely told me their child's name, but I knew there was no child in my room by that name. I definitely would have remembered that name!

"Sometimes he goes by his nickname, Diffy," they suggested. I knew there was no one named Diffy in my room either. I asked if they had checked him into a different classroom. No. This was definitely the room where they left him. I asked my helper if any children had left the room for any reason, and she was sure none had. Everyone was beginning to panic. How could I have lost a child? I was near tears, as were the parents.

Just as I was ready to call for help, a bright, cheery voice called out from behind the toy shelf, "Hi, Mom and Dad." It was Buddy. These people were Buddy's parents. Everyone was completely confused—me, the helper, the parents. Everyone but Buddy.

Buddy explained that no one could say his real name, and if his name were Buddy maybe someone would let him *be* a buddy.

Later that day I thought a lot about the incident and about names. I recalled the passage from Revelation 2, "To him who overcomes…I will also give him a white stone with a new name written on it, known only to him who receives it." Is there power in names? DeVilliers certainly thought so.

Dear Lord, thank you for knowing me by name. Thank you for leading me. Thank you for being my Shepherd. Please help me to lead my students to an understanding of your love and sacrifice. In Jesus' name, amen.

From that day to this, I have been very careful to respect names and to help children do the same.

♥ Locate a book that lists Christian names and their meanings. Find your name in it. Look up the corresponding Scripture passages. Can you see ways your life reflects the meaning of your name?

♥ This week, make name tags for your children and add a name that reflects the best in that child, such as "Aaron—tenderhearted."

♥ Read John 10:2-4. What does it mean to you that Jesus knows you by name? Take a moment right now to thank Jesus for being our good shepherd.

Who's in Charge Here?

Every minute was accounted for—the opening, the worship, the teaching, the closing, the prayer time. I hated having unplanned time. But suddenly a last minute emergency meant I wouldn't be able to lead the class. So I called one of the more reliable young volunteers, Anthony, to ask if he would cover the class. I left all my notes near the door and headed off.

As I left I prayed that Marion, a sixth-grader, would return to class that night. She had been a regular, but she hadn't been to class in several months. I had heard that things were not going well with her family.

When I checked in with Anthony, I was dismayed to learn he had never seen any of my materials and had decided to just "wing it." How could he do that? I had worked so hard. I had everything planned. I knew it was an important lesson.

Anthony quietly told me that Marion had returned and asked if she could talk to us about what was going on in her life. Anthony just let her talk about all the struggles and pain she was

I had everything planned.

89

facing, and then the whole class had surrounded her and spent the rest of the evening praying for all of her needs. I was humbled.

Anthony had been open to what God wanted for that night. Would I have been able to see Marion's needs? Would I—with all my plans and lessons—have been open to ministering to her? That question has radically changed the way I lead my classes now.

♥ My guiding principle in teaching has become Proverbs 19:21. Will you make it yours also? Write this verse on your lesson book, and consult it each week before class.

♥ This week, make room in your plans for the Lord's purposes. Watch for that teachable moment that is not connected to your plan or that student who needs someone to listen.

Dear Lord, thank you for your purposes that are above my plans. Please open my eyes so I can see what you want to accomplish with the lessons that I teach. Do you have another lesson you want taught? Is there someone who needs my special attention? Lord, I submit to your purposes. Help me see those in need. In Jesus' name, amen.

Many are the plans in a man's heart

but it is the Lord's purpose that prevails.

Proverbs 19:21

At Their Level

I felt a little nervous at my teacher's training meeting. I didn't have any children of my own, and I had never worked in a Sunday school class before. I clutched my notebook and held my pen poised to jot down any notes.

"One of the most important tips I can give you about working with preschoolers," said the training leader, "is to get down on their level. It's rather intimidating to be looking up at this huge adult who towers above you."

Soon Sunday came, and I waited for my students to arrive in the three-year-olds' classroom. At first I forgot to bend down as I greeted the children. I wasn't certain it made any difference anyway.

At snack time, I glanced back over my notes and saw the phrase "get down to their level." Suddenly in a moment's quick inward glance, I knew what the little ones must be feeling. I remembered that it had been hard for me to look way up to a big God until I realized that God had knelt down to my level through Jesus. That was when I saw his face and knew his love. God cared enough to come down to my level.

As the children left the classroom that day, I knelt at the door. And as I looked into each of their eyes, I told them, "Jesus loves you." One little girl ran back and, placing her tiny hands on my shoulders, she leaned over and

Dear Lord, thank you for coming down to our level to show us your incredible love. Help me to pass the knowledge of that love on to those I teach. In Jesus' name, amen.

kissed me. She let me know that it mattered that I made the effort to be at their level.

♥ Next time you teach, make a conscious effort to meet the children in your class on their level. Ask them what's happening in their lives at school, with friends, what sports they like. Then share memories of your own childhood.
♥ Read Luke 2:1-20 and Hebrews 1:1-4. What do these verses say to you about God's willingness to come down to our level? How can you share what you've learned with your students? Jot down some ideas as you pray for your class.

"God...knelt down..."

Inspired Memories

If you're involved in ministry, you probably have early memories of Sunday school and the teachers who inspired you to serve. I even remember some of my teachers' names—Mr. and Mrs. Applebee, for example. I remember them as being quite old even when they were my teachers, and I remember their many years of dedication in our church. Other teachers' names I can no longer recall.

But if I could remember their names, I would try to contact them all to tell them that they're part of the reason I'm involved in ministry today. I can't remember my kindergarten teachers' faces, but I do remember how good it felt to help them make fancy folds in the take-home papers and pass them out after class. I remember how great it was to be chosen to help tell the Bible story by moving the characters in the sand table or the big, colorful, felt pieces during the story.

As I got older, I valued having the freedom to ask a question about God if I wanted to. As an adult visiting a new church that was bigger than the one I grew up in, I responded immediately when a teacher came up to me right away, shook hands, introduced me to his wife, and invited me to join their small group. Do you think I even considered joining another small group? Not for a second! I was instantly hooked; I felt accepted and loved.

God knows the needs of the students who walk into your classroom each week. And God prepares your heart to touch their lives, whether you realize it or not.

♥ Take a moment to reflect on your past. Who were some of the positive role models you had when you were the same age as the students you teach? What made you want to be like them? Do you now possess any of the characteristics you looked up to?

♥ Read Colossians 1:9-12. How are you pleasing Jesus? How can you be a spiritual role model for your students? Write your feelings and fears about teaching in the form of a prayer to God.

Dear Lord, thank you for including me in your ministry. Thank you for the students you entrust to me. Please show me how to teach them about you and help me keep my focus always on you and your Word. In Jesus' name, amen.

Heartfelt Thanks Heartfelt Thanks Heartfel

Thanks Heartfelt Thanks Heartfelt Thanks